THE STORY OF
BOATS

GILLIAN HUTCHINSON

Illustrated by
JOHN JAMES

Troll Associates

Library of Congress Cataloging-in-Publication Data

Hutchinson, Gillian, (date)
    The story of boats / by Gillian Hutchinson; illustrated by John
James.
        p.   cm.
    Includes index.
    Summary: Describes the history, uses, and varieties of boats.
    ISBN 0-8167-2705-8 (lib. bdg.)   ISBN 0-8167-2706-6 (pbk.)
    1. Boats and boating—Juvenile literature.   2. Ships—Juvenile
literature.   [1. Boats and boating.   2. Ships.] I. James, John,
1959-   ill.   II. Title.
VM150.H88   1993
387.2—dc20   91-39010

Published by Troll Associates

© 1994 Eagle Books

Design by James Marks
Edited by Kate Woodhouse

Printed in the U.S.A.

10 9 8 7 6 5 4 3 2 1

Contents

Getting afloat

The first boats were probably made from hollowed-out logs. Boats like this have been used all over the world for thousands of years, and still are today.

Early people discovered that light, natural materials, such as reeds and pieces of wood, float in water. They used these for rafts or boats. They also found that a bag of air floats very well and will support weight on water, so they tied blown-up animal skins under rafts to make them float better.

More complicated boats and ships are built by joining pieces of wood. The backbone of a boat

▼ The Vikings were skilled boat builders. They nailed planks of wood so that they overlapped one another and made the joints watertight with hair and tar. This made the hull flexible enough to give against the waves.

▼ One of the quickest ways of hollowing out the center of a tree trunk was to burn it. This was one of the most common ways that early people made boats.

is called the keel, the *ribs* hold the boat's shape, and the planks of the *hull*, or main body, keep out the water.

Heavy materials, such as sheets of metal, sink in water. But if the sheets of metal are shaped into boats, the air inside makes them light enough to float. The biggest ships in the world are made of steel.

▲ Early people discovered that wood floats and will support the weight of a body.

Sailing along

You can make a boat move forward by leaning over the side and pushing the water with your hands. Paddles and oars work even better, because they are bigger and you can pull harder on them.

Long ago, people discovered that if you held up a large piece of cloth, it filled with wind and the boat moved through the water. This sail was soon attached to a wooden pole, called a mast.

Sailboats are clean and inexpensive to use because they take energy from the wind and do not need fuel. But sailboats don't always work as well as we'd like. The wind may blow from the wrong direction, or there may be too much or not enough wind. This means that sailboats depend on the weather. A voyage can take just a few days, or several weeks.

▼ Boating for pleasure today usually means boating without engines. You can enjoy canoeing, rowing, or sailing on many rivers or on the sea.

▲ Sailing ships cannot sail into the wind. They have to "tack," or sail in a zigzag line toward the wind. It is slow, but they make progress.

7

Early seafarers

Although the ancient Egyptians lived thousands of years ago, we know a lot about their boats. Pictures and models of boats — even a few real boats — have been found in the pyramids where Egyptian kings and queens were buried. The Nile River flows through Egypt, so boats were very important. Smaller boats were made from bundles of reeds tied together. Larger, seagoing boats were built from wooden planks.

▼ Sailing ships on the Nile River were beautifully decorated. They had steering oars on each side, which were operated by a man standing at the stern of the boat.

The ancient Greeks had warships armed with sharp battering rams just below the water line. They attacked their enemies by trying to ram a hole large enough to sink them. The more men there were rowing, the faster the ship could go. Greek triremes had oarsmen sitting on three levels on each side of the ship.

▲ Greek biremes were fierce war machines. They relied on the strength of their oarsmen and the skill of the men commanding the boat.

Sails and sailing

Early ships had simple sails, usually square or triangular. Viking long ships had one mast with a square sail. Later shipbuilders began creating bigger ships with more masts, with several sails on each mast to make the best use of the wind.

▼ The Vikings sailed in their long boats from Scandinavia as far as Greenland and Iceland, and probably to America as well.

9th-century Viking long ship

10

Present-day Chinese junk

14th-century Mediterranean trading ship

◄▲ Most sails are made of strong cloth. The sails of some Chinese junks are made of matting stiffened with bamboo. The Mediterranean trading ship has two triangular cloth sails.

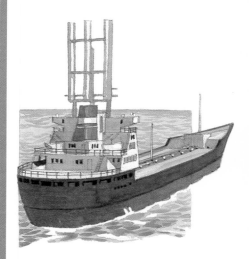

▲ Modern oil tankers are returning to sail power. These sails are called airfoils and are made of metal. They can be turned to catch the wind.

On some ships sailors climbed the rigging to loosen or tie up the sails while others hauled the sails up the mast and pulled ropes so the sails turned to catch the wind.

Sailing is an exciting sport. There have been yacht races for more than 300 years. Today there is a regular around-the-world yacht race. Designers are always looking for ways of making yachts go faster. They experiment with the shape of the hull and sails, and build boats out of lighter, stronger materials.

11

Exploring the world

In the Middle Ages, Arab merchants took exotic goods to Europe overland from Asia. The Europeans wanted to control this trade themselves, so they tried to find a sea route to the East. The Portuguese started by exploring the coast of Africa. They managed to sail around its stormy southern cape to reach India.

Christopher Columbus was more adventurous. In 1492 he left Spain and sailed west across the Atlantic, expecting to reach India from the east. But he reached America instead.

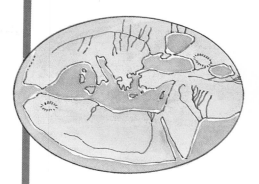

▲ This is a map drawn by a Greek called Ptolemy in the 2nd century A.D. The Mediterranean Sea was the center of the world known to him.

◀ The men who sailed with Christopher Columbus had to be brave and hardy. Some of them believed the Earth was flat and that they might be sailing over its edge. They did not know how long their voyage would be, and conditions on board ship were very hard.

▲ Maps stayed very much the same until the 16th century. When people began sailing beyond Europe and discovering new lands they became interested in mapping. This map shows a greater area and is more accurate than any earlier maps.

In 1519, the Portuguese explorer Ferdinand Magellan set out from Spain to sail westward around the world with five ships and 270 men. He found the route around the southern tip of South America and gave the Pacific Ocean its name. Many of the crew died of starvation and scurvy. Magellan himself was killed in a battle. Only one ship and 17 men returned safely to Spain.

Fighting at sea

Unfortunately, the sea has never stopped people from fighting each other. In the Middle Ages archers shot arrows from wooden castles on the ends of ships. When two ships got close enough, soldiers would board the enemy ship and fight hand-to-hand.

▼ The sailors on these ships were very skilled. The ships often had to move and change direction quickly to avoid an advancing enemy and its fire.

▼ Aircraft carriers are like small airports. Some can carry up to 90 aircraft.

When gunpowder was invented, cannons were put on ships. At first the guns could not do much damage. They only blew holes in the rigging or injured the crew. Then galleons began carrying bigger cannons that could sink enemy ships.

Later ships carried fewer guns, but these cannons were more powerful and could hit a target farther away. These ships were built with armor plating around their wooden hulls as protection against gunfire.

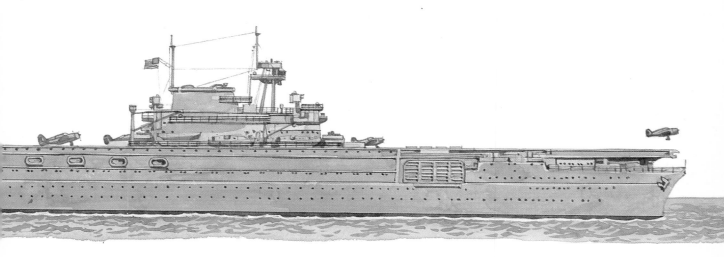

During this century, there has been fighting under and over the sea. Torpedoes fired by submarines can be a great danger to ships. Ships can also be attacked from the air, often by airplanes that have taken off from an aircraft carrier.

Powering ahead

In the 15th century, Leonardo da Vinci designed a paddle boat, with oxen walking around and around to turn the paddle. The hand-turned propeller was also an early invention. But it was not until the invention of the steam engine, which could power the paddle or the propeller, that ships could go much faster.

When the first practical steam engine was built in 1698, it was used to drive the wheels in

▼ This type of paddle steamer was used to sail up the Mississippi River in the United States.

machinery on land. But by 1800, paddle steamers were chugging along rivers. Steamships driven by propellers had more power and were used for ocean voyages.

At first, steamships kept their sails in case they ran out of fuel. But by 1900 ships looked completely different. They had funnels to release steam, instead of masts and sails. Today, boats and ships are usually powered by diesel fuel.

▲ Oxen were often used to make wheels turn in land-based machinery. This idea for an ox-powered ship did not get beyond the drawing board.

▲ The shape of propellers, which has hardly changed over the years, ensures the ship will move through the water as fast as possible.

Carrying cargo

Ships have been used to carry cargo for thousands
of years. Most old cargo ships were big and slow.
They were packed with barrels and sacks, which
had to be loaded carefully so they did not make the
ship unstable. Some cargo, like coal and grain,
was dumped into the ship's hold and carried loose.

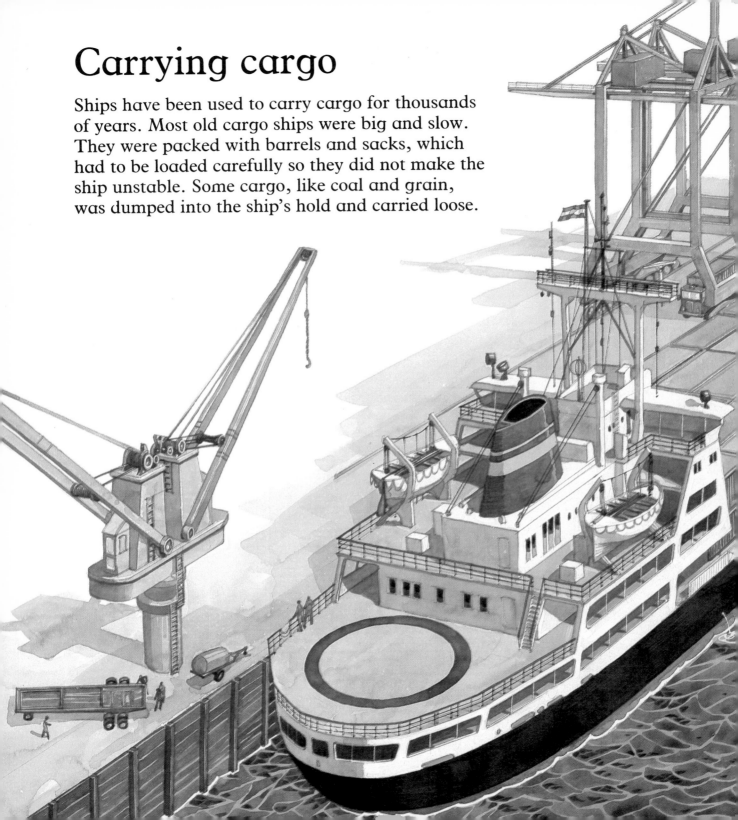

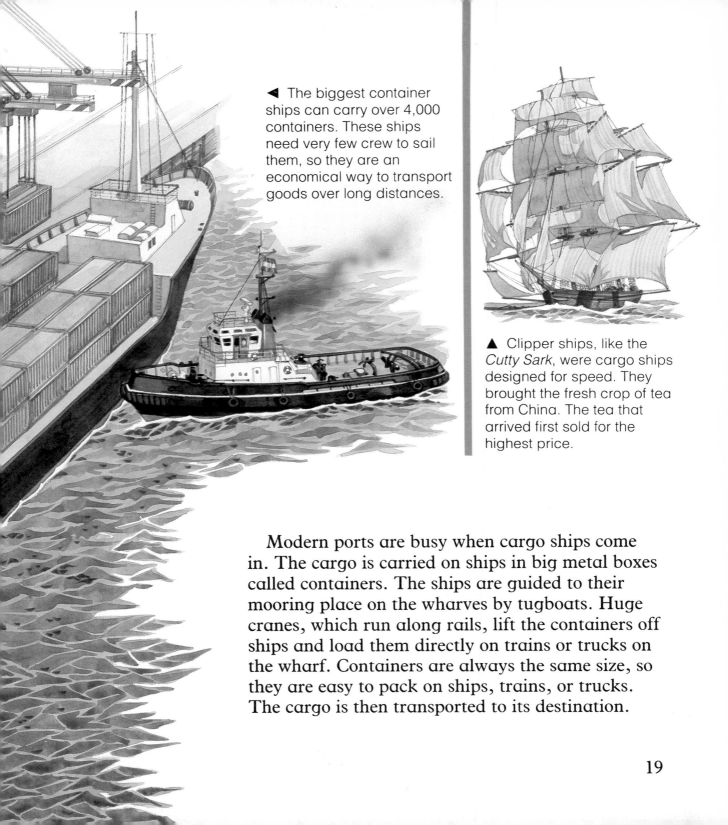

◄ The biggest container ships can carry over 4,000 containers. These ships need very few crew to sail them, so they are an economical way to transport goods over long distances.

▲ Clipper ships, like the *Cutty Sark*, were cargo ships designed for speed. They brought the fresh crop of tea from China. The tea that arrived first sold for the highest price.

Modern ports are busy when cargo ships come in. The cargo is carried on ships in big metal boxes called containers. The ships are guided to their mooring place on the wharves by tugboats. Huge cranes, which run along rails, lift the containers off ships and load them directly on trains or trucks on the wharf. Containers are always the same size, so they are easy to pack on ships, trains, or trucks. The cargo is then transported to its destination.

Traveling below and above the waves

The first submarine was built in 1776. It was called the *Turtle* and was powered by hand. It took almost another century to build submarines that had engines, could fire torpedoes, and could dive rather than just sink. In some marine parks, submarines are used as tourist minibuses. They have big windows so the passengers can look out at sea life.

It was in the 1950s that inventors realized that if a boat could float or hover above the water it would go much faster than one that had to cut its way through the waves and push against the force of the water.

▼ Submarines come in all shapes and sizes. The bigger one is a military vessel, and the smaller one is used for underwater research.

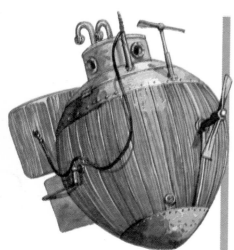

▲ The *Turtle* was like a barrel. One man turned the propeller handle to let water in to lower the submarine, and pumped water out again to make it rise.

▼ Hovercraft and hydrofoils are only used for short journeys, as they are not safe in rough weather.

Hovercraft and hydrofoils both move above water. A Hovercraft blows a cushion of air into the space between it and the water. Hydrofoils have foils like water-skis beneath their hulls.

Liners and cruise ships

Today, most long-distance travel is done by airplane. But air travel is quite new. Until the 1940s, everyone had to cross oceans by ship. Travel took longer then, and voyages to other continents lasted for weeks. Some travelers were in more of a hurry, however, and there were races across the Atlantic Ocean, with a Blue Riband presented as a prize for the fastest liner. People go on cruises today when they have time to enjoy the journey as well as the destination.

▼ For passengers on board ocean liners, the voyage can be a vacation. There are games on deck, swimming, new friends, delicious food, and dancing in the evenings.

The ocean liner *Titanic* was the largest ship in the world when she was built, and said to be unsinkable. Tragically, she ran into an iceberg in the Atlantic Ocean on her first voyage in 1912 and sank. Over a thousand people drowned. Recently, scientists found the wreck of the ship lying on the seabed 2 miles (3 kilometers) down, and sent an unmanned submarine to film it.

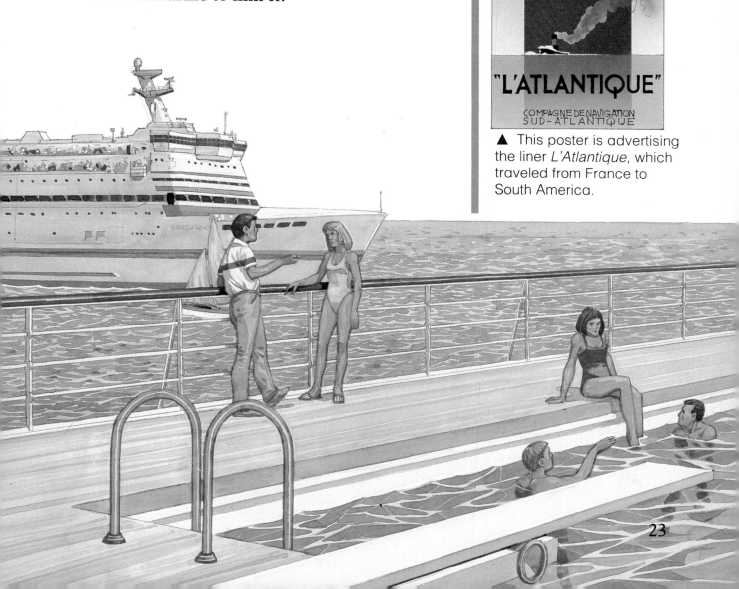

L'AMERIQUE DU SUD

"L'ATLANTIQUE"

COMPAGNE DE NAVIGATION
SUD-ATLANTIQUE

▲ This poster is advertising the liner *L'Atlantique*, which traveled from France to South America.

Work to do

Many types of boats have useful work to do, including helping other craft travel safely. These are the ships of the world's navies that patrol the seas. They try to ensure that the seas are waterways free for everyone to use in a friendly manner.

RX 110

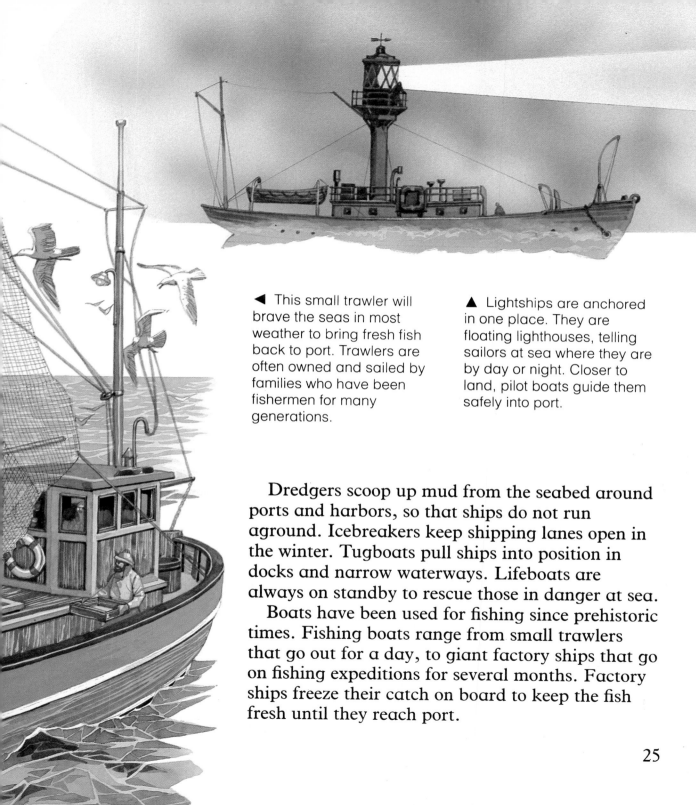

◀ This small trawler will brave the seas in most weather to bring fresh fish back to port. Trawlers are often owned and sailed by families who have been fishermen for many generations.

▲ Lightships are anchored in one place. They are floating lighthouses, telling sailors at sea where they are by day or night. Closer to land, pilot boats guide them safely into port.

Dredgers scoop up mud from the seabed around ports and harbors, so that ships do not run aground. Icebreakers keep shipping lanes open in the winter. Tugboats pull ships into position in docks and narrow waterways. Lifeboats are always on standby to rescue those in danger at sea.

Boats have been used for fishing since prehistoric times. Fishing boats range from small trawlers that go out for a day, to giant factory ships that go on fishing expeditions for several months. Factory ships freeze their catch on board to keep the fish fresh until they reach port.

Living aboard

Some people live on boats all the time. Houseboats are usually moored at one place on a riverside, and inside they are much like any other house, apart from their long, thin shape. People also live on narrow boats on canals. These are not usually moored, so they are like a caravan on water.

Other people live on boats because they are working on them. The life of a sailor a hundred years or more ago was very hard. Living space was cramped, the food was dull, and the discipline

▼ In China many people live on sampans in the harbors and rivers.

hard. Many people died, often from a disease called scurvy, which came from having no fresh fruit or vitamins. Nowadays conditions are much better, but there is usually very little space to spare on a working ship, as most of it is used for cargo, fish, or machinery.

▼ This houseboat looks as comfortable as a land-based home, and you could move and take your house with you.

▲ Living on board a working ship is not always easy. People have to be able to live and work well together.

Just for fun

Boats can be used just for fun, as well as for fishing, traveling, or transporting goods. Whenever the weather is good, people will go out in boats, sailing, rowing, windsurfing, and water-skiing. During the summer most coastal resorts are packed with people eager to go out in boats. They can be small enough for one person to use on a quiet river, or they can be great ocean-going yachts with a crew of about fifteen, with computer-controlled navigation aids, accommodation for everyone, and yards of ropes for hoisting the sails.

▼ Windsurfing is one of the newest sports on water. With a flat board and a sail, you can skim over the water at great speed.

We have sailed a long way since the days of hollowed-out logs. But we must still have respect for the sea. Modern technology may be able to forecast changes in the weather, but it cannot change the weather itself.

◀ Rowboats range from small round dinghies to sleek racers like this one, but whatever the boat, rowing can be fun.

Fact file

Viking explorers

Eric the Red was probably the first European to sail as far west as Greenland. His son, Leif Ericson, sailed further west in about 1000, and landed in what we now call Newfoundland. He discovered grapevines growing there and so called the newly discovered land Vinland.

SeaCat

The SeaCat is a catamaran capable of carrying 80 cars and 450 passengers. In 1990 it made the fastest crossing of the Atlantic Ocean by a passenger ship, taking 3 days, 7 hours, and 52 minutes. It now regularly carries passengers and cars across the Channel between England and France.

▼ This cross-section of a submarine shows that every bit of space is used. Submarines need a great deal of machinery to power them and to enable the people in them to live underwater.

America's Cup

The America's Cup is one of the biggest yachting races in the world. It consists of a series of seven races over about 25 miles (40 kilometers). The United States remained undefeated from the first race in 1851 until 1983, when Australia won. America won the cup back in 1987.

Largest junk

The largest junk was the *Cheng Ho*, flagship of the great Chinese navigator Admiral Cheng Ho. In the early 15th century, Cheng Ho led seven voyages of discovery to many parts of Asia and Africa. On some voyages he took 300 ships carrying 2,700 men. The *Cheng Ho* itself probably had nine masts and was up to 538 feet (164 meters) long.

Riverboat

The Mississippi River in the United States is one of the longest rivers in the world. The *Mississippi Queen* is the largest riverboat. It is 382 feet (116 meters) long and carries passengers up and down the river.

Noah's Ark

One of the most famous boats is the ark that Noah built to protect himself, his family, and two of each species of animal from the Flood. His ark was supposed to be around 450 feet (137 meters) long, with three decks and a door in the side. The longest wooden ship built in modern times was an American ship of 377 feet (115 meters).

▲ In 1947, Thor Heyerdahl traveled on a balsa-wood raft named *Kon-Tiki* from Peru to the Tuamotu Islands in the Pacific Ocean. He wanted to prove that people might have made this journey thousands of years earlier.

Index